MW01199378

Timeless Wisdom from Andreas Moritz

Sage Guidance and Insights – Lovingly Shared

• 978-0-9892587-0-8 Timeless Wisdom from Andreas Moritz paperback (soft cover)

• 978-0-9892587-1-5 Timeless Wisdom from Andreas Moritz e-Book

Published by Ener-Chi Wellness Press ~ ener-chi.com, USA (Nov. 2013)

Book concept: Sunita Kripalani
Book cover design/Tree of Life artwork: Dorrie McKinley

Dedication

Andreas' loving insights and wisdom are timeless; they continue to touch our hearts, expand our thinking, and impact thousands of lives in countless ways from the higher planes.

He is always with us – through the brilliance of his writing, his beautiful healing art, his heart-centered, inspiring messages and all the information that he so generously shared, in order to help us live healthier, happier and more fulfilling lives.

Timeless Wisdom from Andreas Moritz is a respectful compilation of quotes, carefully selected from Andreas' comments and responses to questions posed on his forums or addressed to him one on one. His deep spiritual awareness, compassion and pure, loving essence, combined with a thorough understanding of the human body, have inspired thousands of people to lead more vital, uplifting and balanced lives.

"Open up your heart like a flower in the sun, ask a question in your mind, open this book to any page, and receive your answer with gratitude."

May these words, sentiments and loving guidance continue to provide comfort and warmth, wrapped in timeless support and healing from the heart.

With loving blessings from the Ener-Chi family and the
Ener-Chi Wellness Center,

~ Lillian

I see a bright future for the world, although the transition
we are experiencing right now is not an easy one to go through.
The hurricane of change hasn't even begun, but one day
we will look back and declare, "It's all been worth it!"

Keep your heart open and follow what it tells you to do.
Look for joy and passion in the things you are dealing with.
If something doesn't give you any joy and pleasure,
make the appropriate adjustments in your life that
allow your passion to come forth.

Rules and regulations, and ideas on how life should be lived,
are rapidly becoming obsolete.
It is more about living your own truth, your own wisdom,
your own desires, and not someone else's.

Being on this Earth is your main purpose.
You carry a special code, key or frequency that is
required for the betterment of all mankind.
Your own personal journey, including your struggles,
has a ripple effect throughout creation and is registered,
recorded and used for the evolution of life everywhere.
All this requires nothing other than your simple presence.

Whenever you attend to the body in a caring, loving way,
like you would for a child or pet, the body receives healing.
Cleansing the body is a healing tool and if you keep at it with
loving persistence, the body will open up and begin to respond.
Nourishing it, like you would your child, encourages the
healing response. Seeing the body as your best friend
makes the cells of your body breathe easier and resist less.
Be patient with your friend, and it will come through for you.

I grew up riding horses. These are amazing creatures which,
along with dolphins and whales, uphold the frequency band
responsible for most life forms on the surface of the Earth.
Horses absorb important cosmic energies and
pass them into the Earth through their legs and tails.
The astonishing thing is that almost all horses,
like most dolphins, are aware of the work they are doing.
By interacting with humans, the energies become further amplified.

When sitting on the back of a horse, the human spine
connects and becomes one with the spine of the horse, thereby
allowing the energies to travel in more directions than one.
Humans in disharmony or in need of healing may
feel uncomfortable at first when on horseback
as they release old tensions.

I have personally witnessed great healing in autistic children
when they ride horses, not unlike what happens when they
swim with dolphins. I wish more people could take advantage of this
and spend a little time riding horses, as it used to be
a long time ago, before we had cars.

Regaining health is a great learning process,
a letting go of old, outdated beliefs and values.
There is no need to rush.
Appreciate each moment as an opportunity to
develop your inner power, confidence and wisdom.

A good intention is worth everything.
Each day can be a day of pain or a day of great blessings,
depending on our attitude and how we view things.
See yourself healthy and everything you need will come your way.

Every problem comes with its own solution.
Once found, the problem ceases to remain a problem.
Rather, it becomes a challenge that develops a new skill or gift.
Problems persist when we resist the solution, either through
ignorance or fear of letting go, fear of succeeding, or
fear of loving ourselves. Some of our biggest problems
require more radical transformations in our lives.
If these transformations are accomplished,
the problems turn out to be our greatest blessings.

Be open to accept those changes that you resist most due to fear.
Miracles happen when we step into the unknown.

In reality, all of us, including the animals, and even the
air we breathe, and the birds that sing, are all one.
We cannot divide ourselves;
we cannot separate ourselves from anything.

It is as if the body resists you in every possible way to
heal physically before you have managed to heal the
illusions of yourself, your power, your worthiness.
You can heal yourself by accepting each moment
(even if it is painful) as a blessing, a reason to be grateful for.

Count all your blessings instead of counting your misfortunes.
Don't ignore them, but accept them.
Let them take you anywhere they take you.
You are responsible for them; you allowed them because
you knew that they are in your very best interest.
As long as you fight them as though they are your enemies,
they need to play the 'roles' of being your problems in life.
Give them your blessing, so that they can show their other face to you.

Do whatever *feels* best to you:

simple advice that applies to almost everything in life.

There is the joy of creating things, called passion, which channels
your divine essence into the physical denseness of matter.
Some do this by working with the rays through painting,
for example, while others work on constructing houses.
Some work in banks and infuse money with their energies.
The more pleasure you derive from what you do,
the stronger the effect.
What you do doesn't really matter so much.
As long as you derive some pleasure from doing it,
your essence gets imprinted into it.
Such is the purpose of your presence.

It will become clearer as time progresses what this all means in
relation to the advancement of humankind. Even the beggars
roaming the dirty streets leave their lighted footprints behind.
Being angels in disguise, they are not what they appear to be.

When you stop searching for your purpose,
you start living it more consciously.
Searching for your purpose keeps the purpose itself at a distance.

Only closed hearts can break.
You cannot break an open heart, for it cannot be
insulted, deceived or dishonored.
An open heart can never feel criticized or put down.
If someone appears to insult you or deceive you,
it is only because your heart isn't completely open yet.
An open heart never feels deceived because it can never be a victim
When truly open, you cannot blame anyone for attacking you
because when you don't feel attacked,
how would you blame someone for attacking you?

You can only blame someone for the things they seem to do
against you if you feel you need to defend or protect yourself.
Or if there is an unconscious, vulnerable point inside you
that must be brought to your awareness.
Or an old grievance that you may have had about yourself for
a long time, but never had the chance to accept and resolve.

The deep knowingness that all of life is purposeful
honors and respects health and illness, darkness and light,
wealth and poverty, right and wrong, good and evil.
These are all essential to the evolutionary process of achieving
a higher sense of identity of self that is unlimited and free.

There is no need to superimpose one's truth (transient as it is)
onto another since we are all here to grow from our experiences,
whatever they may be.

The way polarity works, the two sides of a coin are never separate,
even if we only see one of the two.
Negative things in life have just one purpose, which is to bring
its positive counterpart or opposite quality into existence.
Resisting the negative really means that you resist the positive,
for you are not allowing something into your life that
you have co-created for yourself (for a good reason).

This struggle or resistance uses up a lot of energy,
which leads you into a depressed mode.
Depression is actually a recovery phase to help you stop fighting.
Accepting what it provides you with reveals all the secrets about
how you can live in harmony with the Allness That Is.
This is not passive living.
It requires conscious, willing acceptance of what is,
and what you have created for yourself.

When we lose something in life, we only lose it
because it is in our best interest to lose it so that
something new can come into our lives to replace it.
We cannot lose anything that we have not already lost
(which is useless to us).
Loss is part of all natural growth and if we try to cling to
what is about to disappear and are terrified of losing it,
the exciting new possibilities that await us cannot come forth.

We cannot open a new door while trying to prevent the
old door from closing shut and this is true for every life event.
Be equally open to experience the loss of the old and familiar,
and to embrace the gain of the new and unknown, and
life will take good care of everything you need and want.

Everything is well synchronized with everything else.
As human beings, on the surface of it all, we all have a
physical body and seem to be separate from one another.
However, we are more than just physical bodies;
our deepest essence consists of consciousness.
Yet consciousness cannot be divided or fragmented,
because it is one. There is an underlying oneness that
connects everything and everyone with all there is.

The unified oneness that quantum physics describes as
zero-point energy – where all the energies that are
creating everything are consolidated and one –
is not something that exists just on this planet.
In fact, like the trillions of individual cells that work as
one coherent entity, the human body is intrinsically one with
every life form that exists outside our little universe called Earth.

Life is like a river, which flows in varied directions and doesn't complain.
A river never feels like a victim, regardless of the
number of obstacles it may face along its journey to the sea.
There is no real effort in the river flowing downstream or
meandering. Likewise, there is no complaint when
our planet rotates and revolves around the sun.
There is no loss of energy; entire galactic systems move and
expand with no loss of power. The tree doesn't complain that
it has to grow upward against gravity.

There is no effort involved in the creative process.
Being creative in life generates energy and expansion;
there can be no exertion when the creative juices flow.
Do what gives you the greatest joy, follow your passion and
see how effortlessly you become a great success.
This is stress-free living.

Walking the path is your success story.

It is never about reaching the goal, for there is none to be reached.

Living the process is the goal.

If you discipline your child out of love (which is the opposite of fear and anger), he or she will know it and not resent you for it. You will neither feel guilty for that action, nor will you accrue future karma, which is an action to undo any guilt or shame.

When love and compassion are the real motivations behind your behavior, even if someone feels harmed by your actions, there won't be a need for such karmic balancing.
That said, the same action or behavior motivated by fear, anger or resentment is bound to generate feelings of guilt; it therefore requires another episode of karmic return to help bring this inner conflict and self-judgment to a peaceful resolution.

Look to see what you can learn from negative things
without trying to get rid of them.
Embrace everything that comes into your life as a
gift or blessing and it will be that way.

In truth, we are as unlimited and eternal as our consciousness.
This makes each one of us eternal, universal beings.
To wake up to that reality while inhabiting a physical body
is our main reason for being here.

It is part of the game of duality to go from one extreme to the other.
The pendulum swings from one side to the other,
until it finally comes to rest in the balanced mid-point.
Neither side is very comforting, yet while resting in the middle,
which partakes of both extremes without being influenced by them,
one is able to feel the free nature of one's essential self:
it is freedom from fear and limitation.

Conflicts will cease when we start accepting who we are,
including our mistakes, shortcomings and fears.
As we stop rejecting or avoiding our own misgivings and judgments,
we automatically start accepting other people's
mistakes and shortcomings and weaknesses as well.
We are no longer able to find fault in ourselves
and, therefore, cannot find fault in other people.

Our relationships don't need to end up in conflict if
we just take a couple of deep breaths every time
something negative happens to us, for we are
just a breath away from seeing the situation differently.
At each moment, we each have a choice to either say,
"Something bad is happening to me", or
"Well, let me just breathe through this for a while
and see if something positive evolves out of it". . . .

You don't have to react to an unpleasant situation right away;
you can just let it be, even if it is just for a moment.
A moment is just what is needed to alter your perception of it.

Think about the meaning of the Beatles song, "Let it be".
It is a beautiful song which, to this day, touches many people.
It came to us at a time when people felt disoriented and helpless,
when there was disillusionment about life,
and here the band was singing, "Let it be".

By just letting it be, life can take its own course, its own direction.
The river of life can start flowing again without us holding up the strea
Letting things be means accepting them the way they are.
We can then take advantage of everything that happens to us,
both negative and positive.

We are here to learn the art of living.

Life is our lesson.

Some lessons are hard, but they are also our best ones.

Accepting what comes to you each moment as a blessing
will turn it into one and bring joy to your heart.
Rejecting something will create disappointment and fear.

You have free will and choice every moment to
see things differently and reap a different result.

Accept what you don't like and
it will transform into something you do like.
Be grateful for what you already have and
it will attract more of the same.
Resent what you have and it will also attract more of the same.

Such is your power.
It is yours for the rest of your life.

Humans are very complex beings that live and act in many dimensions
of time and space, although most of us are
aware of only this one personality and the body it inhabits.

There are phases in life when we tap into past life trauma
and relive the fear and difficulties to some extent in order to
grow strong in those areas that are not fully developed yet.

It is during those times, for instance, that we may also feel
drawn to ingesting medical or hallucinogenic drugs,
eating certain foods that bother the body, or living a lifestyle
that makes it difficult for the organs to function properly.

All this may then lead to a crisis point which forces a person
to deal with any unfinished business, usually emotional issues,
from the near or far distant past. . . .

Although it may not always feel that way,
all human experiences, including the negative ones,
are in our highest good and never meant to harm us.

The experiences of fear, anger, frustration, impatience and
other emotions are the motivating forces that offer the
opportunity to help us develop, accept and embrace their opposites,
and become more complete within ourselves.

It takes great courage to face our fears,
but it's worth the initial difficulty.
Going through these feelings,
from the beginning to the end until they begin to subside,
is very liberating.

We often make our lives miserable simply because
we are not willing to accept the blessings that we already have.
Many of our true blessings come in the guise of negative events.

Being alone is a test of how well you are able to be free and self-reliant in life. Most people need to go through a period of loneliness in order to be perfectly content with being alone.

Leaning on others to find your happiness may give you a fleeting sense of comfort, security and satisfaction, but usually ends in conflict. The conflict helps you make the right decisions that are best for you at that time in your life. Your soul wants you to be as free as a bird and not locked in a cage, even if it is a golden cage.

If your relationships do not seem to work out for the time being, please consider that this is not an indication that there is something wrong with you. To the contrary, it shows that you are in the process of completing yourself. . . .

To become whole and complete, your soul has arranged to
liberate you from the limitations of all redundant identities,
friends, close relationships, jobs, fears, guilt and shame.

This happens regardless of whether your personality self (ego)
agrees with this arrangement or not.
If you resist it, the energy will be released through the body,
causing inflammation and pain.
The end result will be the same.
But if you let your fears resist what is happening in your life,
physical and emotional pain will take you there.

We all have the choice to see a glass half empty or half full.
You can choose to see whatever happens in your life as a blessing
instead of something bad that needs to be corrected or avoided.

When we feel stuck in a particular situation,
it's often because we feel an obligation to help others close to us.
We are not indispensable, though.
If people you are close to have expectations of you
and you give in to them, then you will feel trapped,
which may affect your own well-being and health.

It is a never a good idea to feed others' expectations;
it only makes them feel helpless and spiritually unworthy.
If they have no expectations of you (which is where it needs to go)
and arrange for finding a way to live out their lives
in a dignified way, it helps them, and you, too.

It is not possible to push emotional issues.
Emotional healing is like the ripening of a fruit;
it takes its own time to come to a point of balance.
Becoming more and more aware of our emotional states,
allowing them to occur, letting ourselves experience them
from the beginning to the end, and recognizing that they
all have a hidden positive reason/element to them,
are perhaps the best ways to deal with them.

Although we may perceive them as bad and negative,
in truth, they are not.
They are here to stay as long as we haven't recognized
why they are really here.
They are often painful, yes, and may need to be painful if we are
reluctant to move on, or are resistant to much-needed change.

At the end of one's rope one discovers that there is new rope.

Life doesn't stop when it ends.

Even death is the beginning of a new cycle of life.

Don't fall into the trap of blaming your doctors if they
fail to help you, for they are not trained to find and eliminate
the causes of disease, or set the preconditions that
the body requires in order to heal itself.
Trust your feelings and inner knowing that your body can help
itself. This is the first prerequisite for healing any disease,
which is but a deviation from the point of balance.

If doctors, friends or relatives instill fear in you to motivate you into
some kind of submissive action or treatment, know that their sense
of reality is fractured and cannot possibly be of any use to you.
Healing cannot occur in the presence of fear.
Seek help only from those who shower you with love and support,
and help you see the deeper meaning and purpose of
what you are going through.
With that recognition, you will be well on your way to recovery.

Letting be what has already occurred develops wisdom. Letting
new things happen when it is the right time helps forge trust in you.
There is no benefit in trying to undo what has already occurred
or trying to prevent what has not yet occurred.
The past and the future exist only in our imagination
and are not based on anything real, but how we perceive them
can turn them into tangible experiences.

For instance, the regret over money you've lost in the past
will likely cause you to lose even more money in the future.
Yet, the acknowledgment that this can help you value yourself a
little more will allow you to receive more abundance in the future.

If you see the best part in the worst people,
they will start to see the same in you.
To be able to see the best in them, you must first
accept, love and embrace the worst parts of yourself.
This is the true secret of peacemaking.

Challenges in life occur only to strengthen parts of ourselves
that we don't feel strong or confident about.
You can only get hurt in areas that are weak already.
The weaknesses in us attract situations that expose our mistakes,
as well as frustrated and shadow parts to give us
the opportunity to grow in self-trust.

The way your life turns out is really up to you.
Once you discover this simple truth,
your life will have the unique purpose you seek.
By living your purpose, you become creative.
Being creative is the only true source of joy and happiness.
If achieving happiness is your goal, it is a meaningless undertaking.
You can never capture happiness.
ople chase it like they would chase a dog that is always faster than them.

Happiness is naturally present when you live creatively and practice or
embody what you came here for, which is to be a creator or co-creator.

It doesn't matter whether you prepare food,
create a painting, play music, make pottery, write a letter,
set up a new business, help others or have a baby.
The act of creating is what is important, not what you create. . . .

If you want something in life, try to find a way to give it first to others.

If it is money you want, give it freely and willingly,

especially when it comes to paying your bills.

At every moment, you have the opportunity to

perceive mundane things as special and meaningful.

By paying your phone bill with a joyful, generous heart,

you can create abundance in your life,

for what you have blessed with joy comes back to you manifold.

And in the same way whatever you send out,

returns to you like a boomerang because

you are the creator of your life and your circumstances.

You are the magnet that pulls toward you everything you love and fea

There are a million ways to create happiness, but none to achieve it.

While love creates happiness, fear tries to hold onto it.

Choose love over fear and you become your own ever-abundant river of

Whatever we seek to become, we already are;
we just don't know it yet.

Sometimes, trying to do too much to get better can backfire
because it makes you anxious.
The fear of not doing enough can translate into contraction
and hardening of organs and systems in the body and
prevent any healing that you might be trying to achieve.
The body heals best when you are relaxed and
allow it to do what it is already doing.

When what you do becomes too much of an effort,
be aware that you hinder the body's healing efforts.
Disease does not have an agenda.
Since disease is merely the absence of health,
fighting against it causes a loss of power.
When you try too hard or struggle to get better,
the amount of energy you spend on this is the
same amount of energy the body needs to heal itself.
Reclaiming that lost power is therefore essential to healing.
Being relaxed in your actions makes them successful,
whereas being tense sets you up for failure.

Liver cleanses are very helpful for those afflicted with anxiety.
The liver is not just a physical organ, but also a
powerful center of connection to our light bodies (which are
more refined than the physical body and made of light rays).
When it is congested, we go into fear. Fear then turns into
frustration, and frustration into anger and anxiety.

Much of the emotional distress you may experience is locked in
the liver (energetically trapped within the tapestry of gallstones).
Unblocking the biliary system in the liver will permit you to more
easily harmonize with your higher nature and your higher self.
This allows trust and joy, instead of doubt and fear,
to run your life's affairs.

We are not here to take responsibility for other people's actions.
It is their choice to make.
But how we respond to how others treat us is our choice to make.
Once we stop resisting or fighting whatever comes our way,
those criticizing us or putting us down will lose their power over us.
We can thank them for giving us the opportunity to become free of
the need to protect our hearts, and free of fear and conflict.

Those opposing us are only enemies in disguise
(true friends and messengers), although they may not
even know they are playing such roles.
That said, this is not an intellectual exercise, it just happens.
Sometimes it takes time to arrive at the 'shift points' in life,
but what is time?
There is no need to force things or manipulate them.
Patiently being with what seems like an obstinate problem is
the fastest way to resolve conflicts and evolve in life.

What you do to the body affects the mind, and
what you experience through the mind affects the body.
The body/mind vibrates according to what it is fed with –
food, information, sensory perceptions and other things.
Choice or free will controls the way we perceive the world.
We become the choices we make for ourselves,
consciously and unconsciously.

Whenever you cannot figure out something, just let it rest
for a while and you will be guided to what you need to do next.
Worrying over things prevents this from happening.

You may benefit from seeing every problem as a potential
blessing in disguise, for that is what problems truly are.
Trying to figure out the "why" behind everything, especially
the things you consider to be obstacles or adversities,
rarely makes you feel any better.
Every time you catch yourself questioning
"Why this?", "Why that?", and "What's wrong?",
just let go of the need to figure it all out.
Trying to figure things out only increases fear and doubt.

Observe what is, let it be, and
the blessing waiting behind it will show up.

It is not important what beliefs you have, but
it is important how you see and treat yourself.
Beliefs are formed in the head and
they require a lot of trust, proof and effort.
The rest is knowingness, which is effortless and joyful.
True knowingness is a matter of the heart, not the head.

What kinds of lives you have lived or what kind of parents
or upbringing you have had is not important.
What matters most in life is how well you love and accept yourself
in spite of all the difficulties you have encountered,
for this determines how your future moments will be for you.
Beliefs cannot secure you a better future than that which
you create by accepting yourself the way you are.

Being physically attractive is not a requirement for
being loved by someone special. In fact, truly special people
are capable of loving those who are not physically beautiful at all.
It takes a person with a deep, loving heart
to find another person with a deep, loving heart.
It is only the shallow and empty-hearted who see
not being beautiful as an obstacle to love.

Many people fall in love with the looks of others,
but not with their soul and heart.
They are likely to become disappointed and lonely,
unless they seek to love another's soul and heart,
not their (fleeting) physical appearance.

When someone loves you for who you are, with all
your weaknesses and gifts, you will know it is for real.
That is the kind of person you want in your life.
You don't need to be perfect at all
in order to be loved in a deep and special way.

It is very easy to feel compassion for nice people, but the
real test of compassion comes when we face angry, unkind people.
Anger can only be triggered in you if the anger is already
inside of you. So when another person comes along
who does something annoying, you become upset and angry.
In reality, though, you don't become angry because of their action,
but because it brings up something in you:
a previously experienced frustration that
never had the chance to become resolved.

The anger is your opportunity to feel and allow it, not reject it,
and which will then permit you to for-give yourself.
Forgiving is the act of 'giving for' yourself
what you've neglected to do for quite some time –
that is, to love and accept yourself with all your heart.
Once healed in this way,
there is simply no way for anyone to make you angry again.

Our response to stress is what makes us stressed,
not the situation or problem that we are facing.

Source Love is who you are without the
associations and attachments you make.
It is the "I" behind "am a doctor/teacher/man/woman/
good person/bad person/etc.".
Nothing can touch the Source Self; it is always free.
The loss of freedom and true joy occurs when we identify with
the roles we play and the things we do, lose or gain.

I consider our Earth to be a living being with whom we can interact,
just like we interact with each other.
When we take from the Earth, we can do this with
respect and gratitude, or we can do it without this attitude.
This makes all the difference.

When the Native Americans used to kill animals during harsh winters
or took from the Earth's natural resources,
they blessed them, demonstrated their fortitude and
expressed gratefulness for what Mother Earth provided.
We now believe that the Earth belongs to us, including the land
we buy. In truth, we are leasing the Earth during our stay here.

If we see the inherent blessings, we cannot help but be grateful.
Our gratitude changes the effects that 'negative things' have on us.
So when we take from the Earth in ways like the Native Americans
used to, our energies enhance the Spirit of Earth, not deplete it.
The more of us who do this,
the faster the process will be of higher-dimensional integration.

Let go of trying, and it will happen.

Trying is a human thing.

Nature doesn't try and yet it accomplishes what it needs to.

Let go of trying and you are naturally aligned with your universe.

Be kind to your body and it will be kind to you.

Nourish it and it will nourish you.

Love it and you will be loved more.

Start step by step:

Make choices when it comes to eating and sleeping, and
your body will reward you with greater well-being and self-esteem.

Your own free will determines which route you wish to take.

When a soul chooses to take birth at a certain moment in time
and in a particular place, it does so because the influences of the
environment and the constellation of the planets at that moment.
These serve as a seed of probabilities that can then
sprout into specific opportunities and challenges that
the person chose to encounter during her or his lifetime.
It's not that there are adverse planetary influences
that can make someone's life miserable.
Planets merely radiate specific vibrational frequencies
in the form of specific energies, some of which appear as
obstacles to slow us down because we need to do that
so we can love and accept ourselves a little more.

Other influences amplify our creativity and happiness,
for instead of needing to learn and grow because of friction,
we also need to learn and grow through joy.
Either way, there is no malicious influence, only opportunity for
growing and getting stronger in areas of weakness.
We radiate our weaknesses and perceived shortcomings
into the atmosphere, and they are reflected back to us
by the environment, planets and the rest of the universe.

There is deeper meaning to be in places and situations
that appear to be non-supportive, not spiritual enough,
not friendly or bright enough.
Many of the more daring souls go into areas that are
dense, rigid, dark and even hostile in order to soften them up
and bring hope, understanding, upliftment and even love
to the people who need it most.

Accept what you have right now as ideal,
for it has been arranged by your higher self for a good reason.
There are no lost times because the only time that exists
is right now. The past is with you always, right now.

You have the choice to see your past as regretful;
this will make your present moment regretful also.
Or you can choose to see your past as one that has been
as good as it could have possibly been, given your karmic
opportunities, and this will make your present moment ideal also.

Make your life your best teacher and honor each part of it,
even the negative things.
The more you accept your weaknesses and mistakes, the more
you will see them as gifts and derive great benefits from them.

With each liver flush, another layer of suppressed feelings is lifted.
With each kidney cleanse, another layer of fear is lifted.
All this may not feel good while being released,
but it is worth it in the end.

You are never punished for anything in life.
Any pain you experience exists so you can heal the areas
where you feel wounded. Pains are always a form of healing
to help you stop resisting what is actually good for you.
You can see the pain as a form of punishment, as some religions try
to tell you, or as a release of guilt (guilt equals self-punishment).
If people knew that their so-called problems are actually
solutions in disguise, they would be more willing to accept them,
rather than resist them.

When you let things pass through you, you are in the flow, and
healing occurs naturally on all levels of body, mind and spirit.
Holding things inside short circuits the energy flow in the body and
mind; this is the ultimate cause of disease (on any of these levels).
Disease is the attempt to let what is kept locked up inside
to come out and, thus, restore the energy flow.
It is quite simple when it comes down to it, yet when the
human mind tries to figure it out, it becomes all so complicated.

God isn't outside you. God is just as much you, in you, and in everyone and everything else, regardless of whether there is the awareness of God's presence or not.
Not even an atom could move from point A to point B without the presence and energy of God.
God is an omnipresent field.
The deepest part of you is also God.

We humans tend to deny our divine nature (we are children of God) and when things are going wrong because of this self-denial, due to fear, guilt and shame, we look for God outside ourselves to save us.

Collectively, we are in the process of realizing that there cannot be lasting happiness for anyone unless poverty, starvation, stressed living conditions and the destruction of our environment are completely rooted out everywhere.

Not feeling accepted or loved results from
not accepting and loving in previous lifetimes.
Being neglected results from having neglected.
Being abused in whatever form results from having abused.
And so one's negative life experiences occur for only one reason:
to balance the two opposites and bring the unfinished business from
the past to a conclusion – a conclusion that eventually
requires full approval and acceptance of oneself,
including all one's "faults", "weaknesses" and "mistakes".

Because of massive global exploitation and pollution,
the being we call Mother Earth is now consciously integrating
with her higher-dimensional essence.
Eventually, this frequency change will only support life forms
and human beings who can harmonize with the new Earth.
Communication will be more telepathic than electronic or verbal.
People will instantly feel something when they hurt someone or
the Earth because they will notice that they are doing this
to themselves, and this will become unbearable to them.

People will either 'check out' or adjust to the new ways of
the Earth. The Earth will work with them and quickly replenish
her natural resources and create new resources because she
will no longer be bound by dense matter and energy fields.
Distorted energy lines will be repaired just as we can
repair damaged meridians in our body.
Every calamity comes with a blessing of some kind,
and we all are challenged to see it this way.

Often, when you feel you cannot live without eating a certain food,
your attachment tells you that you can greatly
learn and grow from your craving.
By not immediately giving into it, you will be able to open your
mind and heart to an inner emptiness that is behind it all.

Feel this emptiness without trying to understand it;
just let it be there for as long it needs to.
This allows it to become transformed into a
sense of fullness and joy, where no cravings can exist.

Notions such as "An eye for an eye", "A tooth for a tooth",
and "As you sow, so shall you reap" are not really related to
external mechanisms of karma returning to you.
Karma means action causing reaction. But action and reaction
are basically the same thing, and always occur inside the doer.
Hence, "An eye for an eye".

If you kill someone, you are not really responsible for the
death of the other person – that is only how man's laws regard it.
Cosmic law looks at what happened before this event and
finds that the victim is responsible for what happens to him.

In a previous life, the roles were perhaps reversed, and
today's victim was the murderer back then.
To bring balance to an unbalanced relationship between the two,
you may agree to do the killing this time so that the victim
can feel what it is like to be killed and, at the same time,
clear up the guilt from killing you in that previous lifetime.
Unless the other person (the victim) truly accepts himself
(a kind of self-forgiveness) and replaces the guilt with
love and compassion for himself and others,
so long will karmic retribution be necessary.

When you feel you have a problem,

listen to your heart with all honesty.

Ask your body how it feels about it.

Perhaps request your higher self to give you some hints

before you go to sleep at night.

You may get your answers in unexpected ways.

Somehow, someone, a book, an insight or inner knowingness

will then give you what you wanted to find out.

Your body, circumstances, people or the world are not your enemy,
and neither are you.
You are not a victim of sorts, but acting as
one who generates the entire drama of being one.
Stop fighting, and accept those parts of you that
deserve to be loved and cherished,
especially those you do not like, and others who do not like you.
Rather than letting your energy go into battling,
you can direct the same energy into loving.

Everything in nature can be healing, but resistance prevents it.
Every person, by nature of his very existence, is a healer.
We all generate an energy field that mingles with
other energy fields of people, plants and animals.
If you feel good about yourself,
then your energy field has an uplifting effect on others;
you bring their energy field to a level of higher vibration.
They may reward you with a smile or thank you for one thing or anoth
This makes you a healer.

When you don't feel good about yourself, your energy field drops
in frequency and you make it difficult for others to maintain theirs.
This may earn you an angry or unhappy reaction.

Life is like a river, it wants to flow and not be held up.
Obstacles cannot last forever.
The river of life will find a way to go around them.
Obstacles sometimes seem insurmountable,
but that is only a figment of our imagination.
If we see something as a problem, it will be one.
The moment we focus our energy and attention on what is possible,
the stuck energy will flow again and offer us
new opportunities or new insights that will
transform the problem into a newly found opportunity.
Obstacles are our friends; they challenge us to
become stronger in areas of weakness.

Without a victim, there is no victimizer.

The victim is always responsible for what happens to him or her.

The moment we realize we are not a victim but a co-conspirator,

we become self-empowered, and at that moment,

abuse can no longer take place.

Only weak people can be abused.

Based on certain past life experiences where someone has

'victimized' others, the soul seeks the opportunity to

become the victim in return, needing to balance out the

previously accumulated guilt and shame of having harmed others.

The weakness and vulnerability in the victim

then become the magnet to pull someone towards himself

who can help that otherwise tortured soul find peace.

Once the balance has occurred,

the feeling of being a victim subsides, and so does the conflict.

Moving to a different place always involves an energetic shift
from certain karmic connections and opportunities to new ones.
And if there is resistance or hesitation, it is good to leave it as it is,
until you feel a strong impulse to move.
If fear seems to be in the way, then that is a good thing, too.
It serves as the motivation to stand up for yourself and
respect yourself as you would respect another.

Our eating habits and other ways we treat our body
reflect what is inside us. A person who neglects the physical body
and focuses only on spiritual matters misses the point.
The body, too, is spirit.
Beyond its molecular, atomic and subatomic manifestation,
the body is energy and information, or pure spirit.
Giving the body the message that it isn't really important
sends the body's spirit (which isn't separate from us) the message
that it doesn't need to function well, and so it won't.

For every problem there is a solution, somewhere.

Powerful "Ah-ha!" experiences (instant recognition) bypass the left brain and open the right brain/heart connection which is the direct way to bring completion to the incomplete, so-called negative and mostly subconscious thought forms, experiences and emotional states.
Mere intellectual understanding may satisfy the mind for a little while, but cannot have a meaningful impact in the long term.

Share your feelings with those concerned simply by
stating what you feel without trying to explain; otherwise the
fear of being hurt by others will continue or even become stronger.
By not being honest with them, you bury the pain inside
and this can affect you both mentally and physically.

Let them have their reactions, if any,
but they deserve to know and you deserve to move on.
It is less about the relationship, and
more about ending years of fear of being hurt.
You cannot be hurt if your heart remains open
and you share what you feel.
You only get hurt when your heart is closed.
It is closed when you are afraid. Then someone must come along
to break it in order for it to open again.

We inherit our own past life experiences and create new ones,
all of which determines the challenges we face in this life.
The challenges are different for each person.
Overcoming the challenges and becoming stronger and wiser
because of them is what awaits us in due time.

Healing is controlled by the body, not by medicine.
A good medicine can be pleasing to the body, which triggers a
healing response (placebo). Food can do the same.
That's why Hippocrates said that food is your best medicine.
Anything that truly satisfies your body (versus just your senses)
makes it whole and healthy. Art, music, nature, fresh air –
all of these can trigger a healing response.

Expressing love to your body, and being grateful for
what it does for you, encourages it to do an even better job.
Telling it how bad a job it does and then punishing it with foods,
drugs, alcohol, long nights and poor nourishment inhibits healing.
The power of healing always lies within you.
When you start practicing it, your world lights up.

For as long as the body is alive and functions to whatever small
degree, it is an amazing feat upon which you can build and expand.

With loving care, attention, self-appreciation and gratitude
for what you have and for what works for you,
you have everything you need to turn your life into
an even greater miracle than it already is.

During moments of despair, giving up hope has no purpose
and just paralyzes the process.
You are sometimes given a challenge, not as a form of punishment,
but as a blessing in disguise to lift you up into self-mastery,
doing things that only few could accomplish.

How we treat Earth when we take from her is more important than
what we use or take. Mother Nature is more than just a bunch of
atoms. She is a living being just as we are; only larger.
She responds to our thoughts, feelings and collective activities
by altering her behavior, weather patterns and Earth movements,
accordingly, to sustain life as best as possible.
When we limit ourselves, she becomes limited, too.
We are like the skin cells of her body.
If we erupt, she erupts. If we calm down, she calms down.

If one sacrifices one's life to please others,
this counts as an imbalance that warrants a correction,
for it can involve conflict and pain.
We are not to be held responsible for the
choices and experiences of others, even our loved ones.
Otherwise, we rob them of an important growth lesson,
regardless of how old they are.
We are here to support each other when it does not involve
becoming fearful or concerned about others.
If we worry about them, it is a good idea to step back and
look at our own insecurities that we project onto them.

Allowing others to have their challenging experiences is love.
Trying to fix their problems so that we can feel less fearful isn't.

Again, it is always good to help others as long as
we don't feel concerned and, therefore, deplete ourselves.
If we worry about others, we bombard them with our
fearful energies, and that doesn't help them, but keeps
reinforcing their dilemmas and causes them to remain stuck.
Assuming responsibility for others is an illusion
that turns them increasingly helpless.
The best help we can offer others is to encourage them to
make their own decisions, without trying to persuade them
one way or another.

Whereas you can learn much from disease and suffering, you can just as well learn through non-painful experiences.

When faced with criticism, see the fear that drives a person

into putting you down or criticizing you.

Criticism is never directed at someone else.

It always reflects the fear of not being good enough.

As soon as you are seeing that fear in another, you may be

helping them, simply by understanding where they are coming from.

It triggers the harmonizing energies of understanding

and compassion, rather than the divisive energies of

defensiveness, anger and irritation.

Sometimes in life, it is important to let a being (human or animal)
die in dignity, and swiftly, instead of prolonging life
just because we don't want to let go.

The higher self or soul of a pet cat, for instance, may have
no more reason to maintain its physical presence here
and has decided to move on and, perhaps,
return to you at another time (as often happens).

Express your gratitude to your pet for having brought you joy.
In return, your pet will be grateful to you for not prolonging its life
and making the transition a very painful one.

There is no "supposed to" in life.
You are in charge of your destiny,
regardless of whether it is
fear and doubt creating what you are afraid of,
or love and courage bringing forth the
realization of your greatest dreams.

Whatever you resist in your life becomes painful.
By accepting and embracing what you resist, you heal the pain.
Disease is a sign of resistance, and it serves to
heal or break the resistance.

Life is a journey that takes you in a circle
just to lead you to the point where you started.
It shows you that you were always there.
This is the importance of the journey.

Answers to questions or problems are hard to come by
when the mind is scattered or focused on problems.
It is much easier to develop knowingness when
the mind rests in the point of self where oneness reigns.
All life emerges from a unified point or field of oneness
and returns to it. You are that field.
But when you focus your attention outside yourself,
you lose perception of the whole.
Life's events are then seen as mere snapshots of
perception and time, instead of a continuous flow of experiences.

Life itself is your guide; you don't need to invent one.

Life teaches you everything,

but your heart must be open to receive it.

Suffering is not due to what happens to us,
but what we make of it, how we respond to it.
Wise people see blessings behind every calamity,
and so each one becomes an opportunity to them.
Others fear 'bad' things could happen to them at any time,
so they attract more of the same.
We choose our parents and circumstances before we are born
so that we can develop greater gifts and abilities,
regardless of how adverse the conditions may be.
Adversity is merely 'added diversity'; it is never against anything.
Our reality is not set in stone,
but changes according to how we perceive it.

Everything is important, everything is spiritual:
even darkness and negativity.
Emotional toxicity arises when we resist something,
when we feel we cannot accept something or
when we feel we are not in our power (victim).
Likewise, physical toxicity arises when resistance builds up in the
body, which is a blockage or congestion, as in blocked bile ducts.
However, toxicity can also arise when the elimination of
toxins or waste from the body occurs more slowly than
their release from a certain area.
To correct that, it is wise to cleanse the three large
organs of elimination: the colon, the liver and the kidneys.

When you don't get along with a person, it is mostly fear of being
hurt that shuts down your heart and ends that relationship.
In truth, there is nothing really to fear.
Nobody can hurt another person unless that person allows it
for some reason or another.
Nobody can deceive or disrespect another
unless the other chooses to feel deceived or disrespected.
The real reason for becoming a victim of sorts is
feeling guilty or ashamed of not being good enough,
right enough or beautiful enough.

You can only attract toward you what you don't like in yourself.
When there is a conflict between two people and you decide
to end the relationship in anger, you won't gain much from it,
except shutting down your heart even more.
It is best to let your emotions rise and fall before making that
decision. Once you are more calm and accepting of what is,
that is the time to make your move.
This will prevent a similar situation from arising in the future.

Taking each moment and feeling as they come,

and accepting them as blessings,

generates gratitude toward everything that happens to you.

Once you see blessings behind everything, you are in your heart,

for only the heart sees the larger picture of things.

By judging yourself,
you automatically attract judgments from others.
By criticizing yourself, you attract criticism from others.
By loving and accepting yourself,
you attract those who love and accept you.

The outer world is your mirror – nothing less and nothing more.
The world treats you the way you fear or love it.
Helping others so that they help and love you
is based on the feeling of unworthiness;
this only causes others to feed off and resent you.

Being kind to yourself is the greatest gift you can give to this world.
It spreads your love and joy to all those who are ready to receive it,
and they will return it to you manifold.

It is not about having a perfect life,
but seeing the imperfections in your life as being perfect.

Problems exist as problems in one's mind only.
Thinking that there are external powers or circumstances
that lay obstacles in your path shows that there is a
need for self-empowerment and self-acceptance.
In reality, victimhood doesn't exist.
You play this role in order to learn to stand up for yourself
and express what is inside you to the outside.
You are naturally weak and gripped by fear only when
you believe or feel there are such things as external threats.

By facing your fears, by doing exactly what you are afraid of,
the fears no longer control you, but you begin to control them.
When you no longer feel controlled by your fears,
your perceived threats disappear as though they never existed.

There's nothing wrong with going down when the wave is going up;
it has to come down.

And if the wave doesn't come down, then it cannot go up again.

Life is made of opposites, but we don't have to
participate in the opposites; we can be in the middle.

Any unresolved relationship issue, where you feel unloved,
not understood or frustrated, upsets Vata
(air, movement, change) more than anything else.
It can shut down digestive functions by forcing blood away
from the internal organs to the bones, muscles and skin.
Also, in women, any unresolved problems in the sexual aspects
of a relationship tend to cause discomfort before menstruation.

It is difficult to heal on the physical level when there is
a basic unresolved conflict of some kind. It requires
courage and trust to stand up for oneself and for one's needs.
If others do not respect and honor you for who you are,
it may be best to walk away.

Disease is the absence of health.
Trying to rid yourself of disease causes you to be
stuck in the notion that there is something wrong with you,
thereby creating a separate reality from who you really are.

You can never be a victim of anything,
for you always create your own reality.
Your past lives are also current lives (parallel realities)
that regurgitate everything you have never completed
(where there is still an opportunity to love and accept all the
things, circumstances and people who were in conflict with you).
In truth, everything that ever happens to you
is in your best interest.
Life is about getting to the point of seeing it this way.
And that can only be a good thing.

If you are afraid of desiring too much, you are bound by fear.

This makes you confused and weak.

Desire with your heart and enjoy everything you desire.

This is the fastest way to harmonize with your higher nature,

for it stimulates passion.

When you feel passion in what you do, you are on the right track,

the track of 'dharma'.

We humans have so much lived by the rules that
we don't much trust our own feelings.
Rules don't make us any safer; in fact,
they instill the fear in us of what comes after we break them.
So many of us remain imprisoned by the idea that
we need to be guided by others, by books, by codes of ethics
and other such rules because we are not
competent or good enough to know what is best for us.

But it is time to break free of all these
self-imposed or accepted limitations.
Let your heart speak for itself and
honor everything you come into touch with.
Everything has value –
good and bad, right and wrong, dark and light.

One doesn't need to fight the negatives of life,
but accept them as opportunities for growth and enrichment;
this helps to transform adversities and makes them useful.
It automatically upgrades negative belief forms into positive ones,
otherwise just making up positive beliefs may be
tainted and undermined by trying to avoid the negative beliefs.

Discovering that negative occurrences are actually beneficial,
and not harmful, makes it a lot easier to be fear-free and to
passionately create new beliefs that feel good.

You have powerful energies inside you that constantly
create your reality. If the perception is that there is
something bad 'out there', then that is what you will manifest.
Hope is the desire for 'something better than....',
which focuses really on the 'than....' and creates more of the same.
Life is about loving everything that happens to you,
and then nothing bad can ever happen to you.
The bad never comes up.

Working too hard toward a goal puts your energies away from where they need to go: the present moment.

Mental and physical health are very much intertwined.
For example, it is very difficult to be content, happy and peaceful
from within if the liver, colon and kidneys are congested.
Likewise, if there is an old resentment or suppressed traumatic
event that has never been resolved, one cannot be happy either.

Then there is a happiness that does not depend on
circumstances, things or the body.
It is state of being where one is grateful, regardless of
what happens in one's life, good or bad – where there is
no need to categorize people, objects, events and situations
into positive or negative, but where purpose is seen in both.

Most problems can be resolved by attending to the inner self.
Making time for yourself, meditating, exercising, eating well,
sleeping well, being in nature and in the sun,
are all ways to nourish the roots of your life.
Each moment of self-acceptance and gratitude is a
way to open the door to the oneness of self.
Each day is a gift, even when "bad" things happen to you.
I learned much of what I know from these so-called "bad" things.

It is not just in one of our other lifetimes,
but in all of them that we live simultaneously.
All lives are staggered together,
but kept from us through a 'veil of ignorance'.
This veil of ignorance is thinning now,
which allows us to live more and more consciously
in the other dimensional aspects of ourselves as well,
without creating too much confusion or conflict within.

We are not just the three-dimensional physical human
we seem to refer to as "I" when we live on this planet;
rather, we are all of our past, present and future,
as well as our higher and lower frequency selves.
When the Bible says that we are the children of God, it means
we are the infinite expressions of the infinite reality that holds
everything together throughout the infinite number of dimensions.

There is no need to hasten one's spiritual progress.
The less you try to speed it, the more easily it occurs.

Although not apparent, every each person on this planet
orchestrates his own challenges, difficulties and problems.
People unconsciously choose situations that
challenge them to take a more serious and deeper look
at themselves, their lives and their purpose.
If they cannot do this in a gentle, easy and effortless manner
(there are plenty of opportunities in life to progress in this way),
they will then allow things to happen
that makes them feel pain, agony and suffering.
This generates fear, and to cope with the fear and to 'protect'
themselves, they may either internalize it and get sick and angry
with themselves, or externalize it and project it onto others,
while also becoming sick and angry, directing the anger to others.

If you resonate with their fear,
you may experience similar effects as they do.
You don't need to do this.
You can choose to follow the path of love and trust, and
you will generate more of the same qualities in your life.

The quality of sleep is often determined by what we do during the day. Going to bed with unresolved issues can greatly affect sleep.

More and more people are now becoming aware of their past lives.
They are given the opportunity to see some of their past actions
to better deal with their current life's challenges.
Seeing our own past 'imperfections' can help us
let go of judgments we make of others.
Becoming aware of any guilt or shame for no special reason
is often related to us having killed others or
harmed them in some way lifetimes ago.
The guilt forces us to play the role of a victim, or feel unworthy.

Eventually, we come to a place of self-forgiveness or full self-
acceptance, which releases all accumulated guilt of wrongdoing.
When self-love has been achieved,
animosity, victimhood and conflicts will be gone, too.
Thus, dealing with our dark nature can help us
integrate our divine nature and
arrive at a place of peace, freedom and unconditional love.

Your experiences are not something you need to be afraid of.
It is part of the process of human awakening.

The ups and downs of life make up life.

The down part is equally important as the up part.

The accepting person doesn't perceive the down part as bad,

and therefore cannot suffer.

He is not a victim anymore, and has no more adversities.

Everything is welcomed as an opportunity.

Life is an ongoing experience and its
many challenges may not always make sense to us.
But when you look back in time you will realize that
those challenges were needed for us to evolve and grow,
to take us into areas we would otherwise have avoided going into.

You cannot hurry things and get to a place
where you would rather be.
It is not about reaching goals in life;
it is about mastering and fully living the process of getting there,
no matter how difficult it may appear to be.

People are often hard on themselves because
they do not accept their weaknesses and faults, and
want to get rid of them as if they were pests.

Mistakes are there to teach you to accept and love yourself
more fully. Self-criticism and denial are hard for the body's cells
to swallow. They think you don't love them, and
this undermines their performance.

If you want to make any changes in your life,
don't make them out of guilt, but out of joy and passion.
Otherwise, all you will reap is more guilt and
a lot of disappointment.

Conscious decision-making, intellectual understanding

and trying to figure out relationship problems

cannot touch the subconscious programs.

But the moment one feels in his gut that what he thought was a

bad, negative situation is actually an opportunity –

a problem in disguise, a blessing or a gift one can be thankful for –

the program becomes neutralized.

For instance, when a person truly feels that their cancer is a

great blessing or a healing process, then the cancer can vanish.

Otherwise, the cancer continues to be necessary to

hopefully get the person to that state of mind and heart.

Karma is your own making and, as such, doesn't hold you back.
It only provides opportunity to grow strong in areas of weakness,
master the ability to be free of judgments and
undo energetic patterns from the past (including past lives)
that are no longer in your highest good.
Karma means cause and effect – you reap what you sow.
It is not meant as punishment for sins committed,
but as a way to remove the shackles of ignorance.

Karma is an opportunity.
If seen negatively, it will have negative effects. The negative effects
can become so strong that eventually one gives up fighting it.
This is another way to develop peace and freedom.
If seen positively, karma opens doors for you.

We can certainly be our own stumbling block or downer
if we choose to focus on what doesn't work in life.
Likewise, we can facilitate our own resolution to these
perceived annoyances and hardships,
as being our own strongest assets, if we dare to
accept every detour and use each one for our own benefit.

Once your body is clean it will naturally be drawn to foods that
maintain this clean condition. When the body is congested
and toxic, it craves foods that congest the body even further.
Eventually, you will like only foods that are really useful
for your body and be turned off by those that are not.
This makes sense, since all living species in the world
behave this way, eating only foods that are
conducive to their growth and well-being.
We weren't meant to read manuals and food lists
to know if certain foods are good for us or not.

How others treat you is none of your business.
If you make it your business, you make their misery your own.

A disease is a healing process,
and fighting it only makes it last longer.
You can learn and evolve from any disease,
if you are suffering from one.
The more readily you can accept it as a healing process,
the faster it will disappear.
You can make the best of it.
It can lead you to full empowerment of self and self-love,
perhaps for the first time or once again.

We naturally attract so-called negative circumstances or people into our lives when we foster such beliefs that we are not good enough, shouldn't have made this or that mistake, don't look beautiful enough to be accepted and loved by others, should be smarter than we are in order to be able to complete, or try to be different than who we actually are.

Subtle programs in the subconscious mind are brought into the conscious realm by these 'negative' circumstances and people in order to help bring more awareness and attention to them. There may be the temptation to try to change yourself and fix these problems by being positive (using the power of positive thinking), but this just attracts more such negative experiences.

It is not about trying to become a better person, but to lovingly accept who we are, especially our weaknesses, mistakes, lack of beauty and other shortcomings. Negativity is not a curse but a gift in disguise, including disease and calamity. We can learn and grow through every situation in life if we accept it first, which naturally alters our perception to one of joyful expectation. Once this perceptual 'mode' is in place, we will attract more of the same.

Place your right hand over your heart and ask your heart
to give you a "yes" or "no" answer to what you want to know.
The first impulse is the one to go by.

Focus on creating something, anything.
Even doing mundane things can be improved upon.
The joy of creating is the reward and fulfillment that we seek.
Looking forward to achieving a goal that we may or
may never reach is stressful at best.
To make your life dependent on achieving goals
instead of enjoying the path of getting there
will leave you unfulfilled and empty-hearted.

Your drive to fill yourself up with something outside yourself
is based on an inner emptiness that only *you* can fill,
not anything or anyone else.
When you create something, even if it is just a simple smile
in another person, you are truly filling your heart with joy,
something that cannot be taken away from you ever again.

The main precepts for expressing our spirituality are
self-care, self-love and the fulfillment of our heart's desires.
This is when you are in alignment with yourself –
being of spirit, spiritual.
There is nothing more to do or to be than that.
If everyone did this, we would have no conflict,
no fear on this planet – only love, peace and harmony.

If you truly accept and love yourself, regardless of your flaws, your natural instincts will guide you in your choices of food, lifestyle, exercise and relationships. These will mirror the caring, loving relationship you have with yourself.

It is better to have old memories surface and to face them and let them fade away, rather than keeping them shut tight in a 'dark room' of your subconscious. They are not there to haunt you, but to release you from the judgments of your past. If it feels as if they are haunting you, it is only because you still perceive them as negative, whereas in truth, you are the creator of your own life experiences, and you do this for the sole sake of evolving and expanding your possibilities.

Once you begin to perceive the past events in your life as blessings, you will automatically release these ghosts of memory. You can make that decision at every new moment by insisting that there must be a positive counterpart to everything negative.

Making peace with your past is the secret to freedom, or what you call "liberation", for this will also allow you to see everything in your present and future as divine gifts, which you can only be grateful for. Being truly happy and peaceful is the product of how you perceive yourself and your past experiences.

Bless and be grateful for everything that has happened to you. Be grateful for your hope that the fear that something bad will happen to you again will disappear. Also bless and be grateful for any 'negative' circumstances that fear may be magnetizing into your life.

There may be an opportunity for you to grow stronger in areas of your heart that are still intimidated by unpleasant situations. You may be able to see beyond appearances and view the pain and fear that make some people aggressive and cold-hearted, thereby developing a greater sense of compassion within yourself. When this happens, your heart expands, growing strong and rich.

Accepting what comes into your present moment instead of fighting it removes fear and changes the effect it has on you.

Sometimes, resistance comes up to test your degree of will –
how much you are willing to go beyond your comfort zone
and open up new gifts and opportunities in life.
Behind every resistance lies opportunity.

Who are you? It is not important to find out
what you are here to do, but to find out who you are.
Unless you accept yourself the way you are, you will not know
who you are, and your purpose here cannot be revealed to you.

Be grateful for the little, insignificant things in your life,
for they are your doorway to discovering who you are.

Seek and discover the precious purpose in life's adverse situations
and the rest will unfold automatically.
Don't look for the purpose of your existence.
Looking for it means that you are looking for it outside yourself.
The truth is that you are your own purpose.

Take your weaknesses one by one and show them to the world,
and you will see them disappear.

Once your fear of food begins to lessen,
your absorption of food will increase.
Many people blame their body, organs and glands for
not performing well or causing them trouble.
True healing cannot occur under these conditions.
It happens spontaneously when such a
self-fulfilling belief is released.

Sometimes we are challenged to develop more
acceptance and patience, as these are
both more important than achieving goals.
How can we learn to become more patient and accepting?
When things don't move fast enough or when they don't happen
at all, it is good that we fail from time to time, otherwise
these important characteristics of life are not developed.
Ultimately, we recognize ourselves always to be in the
right place at the right time, no matter what happens.

Physical, emotional, and spiritual issues occur at the same time,
although one may be more pronounced than another.
Cause and effect is an illusion of the mind and senses,
which includes the factor of time.
Yet, since time is not real, but a by-product of our
imaginations prompted by the experience of space and time
(Einstein's Theory of Relativity), no event can truly cause another.
Time is ALL TIME.
So dealing with emotional issues means you are also dealing with
the other two at the same time – physical and spiritual.
Dealing with the physical issues also means that
you are dealing with the emotional and spiritual ones.

You bestow power upon everything you perceive.

The decisions you make are the ones that you are
supposed to experience. The ones you didn't make
in the physical part of your life and are regretful about
took on a life of their own and manifested themselves also,
but not in the third-dimensional world of your physical life.

Often, cleansing one's body, especially the
liver, kidneys, colon and lymphatic system,
is one of the most powerful and effective methods
to achieve emotional balance and well-being.
It is an act of self-love.
Self-love can be a powerful healer,
more powerful than purely physical treatments.
By attending to the body's needs in this way,
it no longer has the need to struggle and survive;
anxiety, innate fears and insecurities subside.

We often process many lifetimes at once.
The different roles that we play, and the experiences that we have,
are directly linked to bringing to completion the 'unfinished
business' from several simultaneous lifetimes that we may call 'past
lives'. At the same time, being here with so many other souls, there
is a 'field effect' to this that nobody can avoid being affected by.

There is a tremendous collective cleansing going on,
induced by ever-increasing energies of a high-frequency nature,
and this brings to the surface any fear, poor self-perception,
insecurities and resistances.

When the pressure gets very strong, there will be a breaking point
or collapse of resistance. This is called a breakdown.
The breakdown lifts you up to a higher frequency of
your own being, until more of you also reaches that level and
clears any resistances (guilt, shame, resentment).

This is what is happening right now, and everyone sensitive and
committed to self-improvement will be challenged to move in
this direction. Those who are not may have an easier life,
but will remain in a denser form of consciousness.
Those who go through it now will have it much easier later
when the world moves into greater disarray and confusion.
They will help those who are going to be desperate.

Don't be afraid of breakdowns, they are the breakthroughs
to propel you into the new, emerging you.

When you feel that a particular organ of your body is 'on strike', you basically mean that the cells of that organ feel disconnected from the rest of the body – perhaps like disgruntled workers who do not get their regular paychecks, which are Chi (energy flow), nourishment and love.

Talk to your cells and let them know that you love them and support them, and that you want them to come back to work. Cells are made of molecules and atoms that follow the blueprint outlined in the DNA. The DNA responds to everything in the environment, including your thoughts and feelings. Any unresolved conflicts in your life affect the DNA and the organs, and undermine the natural healing response.

Holding on to anything in life is akin to missiles targeted at one's body. An organ doesn't just give up functioning without a reason. Health issues are an opportunity to grow strong in areas that are not yet developed, areas where we feel weak or inadequate. Knowing this changes the energy and the DNA's perception of how you see yourself. Your problem is a solution in disguise that can heal something much deeper than just one organ.

The moment I say "no" or "I can't" or "that's tough" or
"I have another problem", I choose to be a victim.
But the moment I say "yes" or "I can" or "I will do my best" or
"there must be a way out of this", I am a victim no more.

If your eye is blurred, your world will appear blurred to you.

There is no external force that carries karma to you.

All karma (action and reaction) is inside you.

Whenever there is guilt or shame left from what you may

have once conceived to be your bad or evil actions

(which is but an illusion), in order to free yourself from

self-strangulation, you will require external threats, unfortunate

events, or circumstances like accidents or antagonistic people

in your life in order to cancel out this guilt or shame.

It is your own seeds that you are putting in the soil.

What you reap is nothing but how you treat yourself,

and not necessarily how you treat others.

If anyone who crosses your path suffers as a result of your

actions or behavior toward them, it is but their own making.

If you feel guilty for what you have done,

then it is your own making.

We are, therefore, responsible for everything that happens to us.

When you are most desperate, there is always a door that will open for you. You can trust in that.

It is always good to have an open mind about the things
we don't know; otherwise we may never grow or expand in life.
Reality is structured in consciousness.
How you decide to see it is up to you, and
this is the only thing that shapes your reality.
There can be no other truth for you except
the one you decide to believe in.

Imagine what you wish to do or have, and give gratitude to it, as if it has already happened, because energetically, it already has. In due time, it will come through for you if it is in your highest good.

The most important thing one can do when hardship strikes
is to embrace and accept it.
Once fully accepted, you will learn from it, discover why it
came into your life, and discover the positive reason behind it.

There is no journey of self-discovery.
I lived in India, I had gurus, and I worshipped and tried to get
through meditation to that state of enlightenment – until I realized
that you are already there before you began your journey.
You don't have to look outside of yourself to find it.

You cannot 'find' yourself because the moment you try to
find yourself, you have a concept of who you are going to find,
and you are 'lost'. You are basically lost to yourself.
It is the learning or accepting who you are that takes you
instantly to the state of enlightenment because then you
realize you can be imperfect, weak and have your faults.
If you have no judgment about it, if you accept yourself the
way you are, it puts you into the space of being: being-ness.

The greatest lesson in life is to let things happen as they unfold
and to know that what has already occurred
is the best possible situation that could happen.
Trying to change it can lead to complications that require us to let
go of the effort we put in to make things move into balance again.
Sometimes we are unable to see the perfection
behind the imperfections of life.

Emotional and spiritual factors have the most powerful influence on our physical health and DNA. All root causes of ill health begin with self-judgment, especially if it is unconscious.

Conflicts in relationships will virtually be absent if we start
accepting who we are, if we accept our own mistakes, our own
shortcomings and our own weaknesses, and if we start accepting
other people's mistakes, shortcomings and weaknesses as well.
When we no longer find fault in ourselves,
we cannot find fault in other people, and
then our relationships will not have any conflicts.

Past lives are no less in the past as this present moment is. They simply occur in other timelines or time dimensions that we call "the past". Usually, karmic past life incidents don't come to the surface of a person's attention before one has reached a certain age. The purpose of karma is to grow through one's past experiences, which cannot be expected to happen in the first few years of life when consciousness is not yet differentiated enough.

All it needs is a trigger to help take the soul memory and translate it into cellular memory. This allows you to physically feel the memory as an emotion – for instance, a fear of something like the fear of drowning, death or losing control, among other fears. The emotion gives you the opportunity to deal with the karma, then pass through and transcend it and, finally, free yourself of the underlying fear. When I did Sacred Santémony for people, I was often able to help complete that process, or at least accelerate it (to closure). People have reported to have lost their fear of heights, or water, or flying after these sessions because we brought an old cycle to a conclusion; hence, the fear was no longer necessary.

Much of our deep-seated fear and insecurity tends to be acquired
during the first few years of life when we are less conscious.
The subconscious, like a tape recorder, records all experiences,
conversations and behavior of our parents and
other adults around us, recording statements such as,
"Leave mom alone", "Stop nagging", "Don't be a pest",
"You are not good enough to be an artist/singer",
and the emotional responses to them.
The child records all beliefs and perceptions and then
replays them later in life, usually after the age of six.

Your problems in life manifest from resistance to what is.
By seeing it with new eyes and letting it happen,
the resistance melts away and so does the problem.

If you criticize me and I don't feel criticized, there is no harm done.
However, if I criticize you and then I, myself, feel unhappy
because I felt the need to criticize you, that has everything
to do with me and it then becomes my business.

If someone criticizes me, it becomes their business, not my business;
it's their unhappiness that they are projecting and
maybe I can help them. I can put my hand out and say:
"Is there anything I can do for you? Maybe you are
going through a difficult period in your life?"

I don't have to counterattack them.
They are unhappy about something in themselves because
only unhappy people can put down other people.

It is important not to pressure other people into doing
what they are afraid of. The choice must be theirs.
When they are ready, they will face that fear and pass through it.
There is a lesson in everything we do, or don't do.

Disillusionment occurs when part of you awakens to a
deeper meaning and perspective of yourself.
It is a dying process where the old life, beliefs and values
lose their attraction, meaning and purpose.
Even a soul experiences darkness – 'the dark night of the soul' –
where the motivation and will to live are minimal,
and everything else becomes 'superficial'.
The question arises: "What is the point of all this?"

However bad things appear to be, everything has a good purpose
behind it. The old self has to die before the new self can emerge.
Like a snake gliding out of its old skin,
life doesn't end with the shedding of the old skin.
The collective drama that is unfolding in the world right now
adds more pain and challenges to this confusion.
The degree of the confusion indicates the
degree of inner transformation.

Although there is light at the end of the tunnel, it is
best not to see the light while going through the process.
Don't judge yourself during this time;
just accept what is happening.
Just as when traveling in a train, you may not realize how fast
you are going, even though you are moving quite fast. The world
is changing rapidly and is turning upside down, and so are we.

If there are things you are afraid of expressing and saying to
others, it is important that you share what is going on inside you,
especially with those who you feel won't understand you.
Become aware of those things you are afraid of expressing
and practice expressing them verbally to yourself,
so that it becomes more conscious.

Thousands of years ago, we lost our telepathic and time travel abilities – moving freely back and forth in time, and in and out of dimensions – something most of us can currently do only during our sleep or dream states. But every moment a new child is born with telepathic gifts (and there are so many now), the collective consciousness moves up a notch in frequency, allowing more and more of us to access our old gifts of telepathy and time travel.

As telepathy and time travel will become part of life on Earth again, people won't misunderstand one another anymore and conflict will cease to exist. It is true that we constantly converge with other lifetime experiences. Why do people feel such a strong calling to go to certain places, far away from home?
Because they feel homesick, wanting to go back to
what still is 'home' in another parallel timeline (or past life).

Why do we suddenly want to be around certain people we meet?
Because we connect with them in parallel lifetimes
or what we call "past incarnations".
The attraction is an old one that now recurs.
We often hear people say,
"This feels as familiar as an old pair of shoes".

We all live different realities, but don't realize that they are all mixed up and overlap. This will all change, though, and we will experience life in a very different way than before.

Being born into a human body feels more like being put into a strait jacket, and dying feels like being released from it. Everything in this world is exactly the opposite of how we perceive it, and it is for us to see both the illusion and the real thing, and not have a problem with either of them.

Although the goal remains the same,
we are responsible for choosing the path that leads us there.

Life itself is a process of transforming one's fears, worries,
doubts and other emotions into their opposites.
When this happens, what was perceived as a threat before
is now no longer threatening.
The so-called negative situations in life, which we tend to see
as problems, are simply modes of perception or points of view.
Since you are the point that is doing the viewing,
you can consciously decide what you want to see
when you encounter a problem.
The effect that results from 'your view of your viewing'
is your own making.
In other words, if you see a certain situation as a problem,
it will assume that reality for you just by seeing it that way.

You are never a victim of anything, even if it appears that way.
There are always choices to be made. You can choose to
cleanse your body, and heal your emotions by doing so.
You can eat healthier foods and your emotions will reflect that.
And if you don't want to do that, don't punish yourself;
instead be happy that you just exercised your free will.

Look for the positive element in every negative thing;
you will always find one. Then dwell on it.
You will discover that all your life's experiences suddenly will make
sense to you. All the pieces of the jigsaw puzzle will come together
and create the larger picture, your life's purpose.
Before long, your self-value will have increased a thousand-fold.

Facing death while still being alive can greatly enrich us. It is one of the greatest masteries to lose the fear of death and dying while you are alive. It leads to the knowingness that death is actually birth, and being born is more like dying.

There is a sense of urgency in the air or ethers
to move into a new, higher state of consciousness and
to start a new life that is based on inner freedom and power,
versus outer dependency and weakness.
The world as we know it is in the process of dying off and
re-emerging in a different form that won't tolerate
people who are not in their power and are not free.
A lot of people now are suddenly trying extra hard to
catch the train that is leaving the station,
and you may be one of them, too.

The focus is on the body right now,
for you will need to be healthy enough to endure the run
or the transition into the new you and the new world.
Your body and the body of Mother Earth now react strongly
to any remnants of discord, conflict, disharmony and
other forms of weakness, to help release and heal
the feelings of guilt and shame from one's past
(including past lives). . . .

The world as we know it is coming to an end and the
cycles of time (seconds, minutes, hours, days and months)
are literally speeding up to allow us to process all the
unfinished business we brought with us into this life stream.
Time seems to be running short in this field of life
and will become even shorter.
It has changed so dramatically that we effectively
no longer live in the present, but a few years ahead in the future.

The quickened years in between brought huge challenges to
individuals and to nations at large,
and karmic retributions are hugely intensified.
The 'new world' will not be based on the past or karma
(cause and effect), but on the power of love and oneness.
Because of this, we are in for a tough ride,
one that can bring out the best and the worst in us,
depending on how much groundwork we have done.
Therefore, some people now feel that
there is almost no other choice but to
make the necessary life-altering changes or shifts.

Pharmacological drugs don't heal; all they do is suppress the surface symptoms and leave the underlying causes intact. If you really wish to heal, then a completely new approach may be your best choice. The liver cleanse is certainly a powerful means to help the body heal itself.

There are no limitations out there other than those you believe in.

You create what you expect.

If deep within, you expect failure,

then following rules is not what you need.

Healing cannot be forced, no matter what we do.
There lies great power in letting things be the way they
have occurred, and observing with curiosity and awe
how events unfold, because nothing that happens to us
is ever wasted or without a deeper meaning or purpose.

I personally acknowledge the presence of chemicals in foods
when I eat out, whether at home or during my travels,
but I am not afraid of them.
Instead of seeing how much harm a certain food could do to me,
I imagine how much good it will do me.
To surround and penetrate my meal with my own energy field
and thought-power, I simply express my gratitude to the food
(silently or vocally), thereby raising the food's energetic value.

When people say things like, "I love this food" or "What a wonderful
meal this is!", the food becomes much more digestible.
It is not just the love energy and skill of the cook
that makes the food so 'special', but also the
positive energy transmitted by the person who eats it.
If the cook doesn't cook the food with love, as it happens
in most restaurants nowadays, the food will not vibrate on a
high enough level to create health and vitality in the consumer.

However, you can 'rescue' the food by exposing it to
your own loving energy. If I happen to eat something
that I know has lost all its energy or goodness,
I just place my hand over it for a few seconds and say,
"Thank you" or "I love you" to the food as I chew or swallow it.

Intuition is the ability to know the connectedness of things, times and events.

All problems can be resolved, not necessarily by working on them,
but by seeing them from a different angle.
Each one is an opportunity for growth, and the problem
usually dissipates when the resistance to it goes away.

When someone loves you for who you are,
with all your weaknesses and gifts, you will know it is for real.
That is the kind of person you want in your life.
You don't need to be perfect in order to be loved deeply.

There are changes taking place on Earth that are affecting
people's personalities and behavior right now. It is becoming
more and more difficult for people to keep their emotions inside.
Many try and they develop cancer, diabetes, heart disease and other
conditions. Some people, instead of attacking themselves in this way,
lash out at others for basically the same reasons.

All in all, it is a time for cleansing of the body, mind, emotions, behavior,
belief systems, lifestyle, eating habits, our relationship with food and
our relationship with the Earth itself. The speed at which this is all
happening is simply mindboggling, but it is in everyone's best interest.

Nobody who seems to be harmed is really harmed,
but a belief of being hurt brings out a suppressed old facet
of one's personality that is ready to come to the surface.
People don't hurt others; they only hurt themselves
in order to break down false conceptions of guilt and shame.
They show up as victims that seek out others who offer to
pull the trigger and raise their hands against them. . . .

There is no reason to be afraid of anything that is currently happenin
for it is all part of the larger picture of things,
a picture that will bring love, peace and prosperity
to those who are ready and willing to receive it.
Nobody will be left out, regardless of whether they
remain in the physical form or not.

To create a beautiful world, everything that isn't beautiful
must be transformed, however long it may take.
We are right in the middle of this phase,
and it may become much more intense;
but with it comes the opportunity to learn and grow spiritually
in ways we have never been able to grow before.

We often answer our own questions by stating them.
As it so often happens, a question contains its own answer,
just like a seed contains its flower or tree.

Learning by rote and trying to remember what you have learned is an outdated form of educating the young, and involves a lot of effort on behalf of the brain, which is not supposed to be that way.

The most creative and successful people in the world didn't use the left brain to achieve their goals, but their inherent creativity. Overusing the analytic part of the brain dulls one's creative genius and is a source of stress and depression. Why are so many young people rebelling against this kind of pressure? Because it is so unnatural. Real education comes from within.

If someone doesn't accept you for who you are, it is their problem.
If you believe your life depends on their approval of you,
then it is your problem.
Not standing up for yourself, your choices or your opinions,
but remaining afraid of criticism, is a major source of depression.

Life is an ongoing experience and its
many challenges may not always make sense.
But when you look back in time you will realize that those
challenges were needed for you to evolve and grow, to take you
into areas you would otherwise have avoided going into.

Falling down during your first months of trying to walk may appear
to be a frustrating experience if you happen to see it that way.
But you can also see the falling as a
way to gain self-confidence and strength.
A toddler who is constantly held by his parents
when he is about to tumble and fall will lack self-confidence
throughout his life and always be afraid of falling,
whereas a toddler who is getting back on his feet without help
will carry that achievement throughout his life.

Jesus once said that what you hold inside yourself will destroy you.

So start expressing your feelings more and show them to others.

Let them know your vulnerable side, your weaknesses,

your mistakes and flaws.

They will appreciate you even more for it.

When expressed, the fears won't affect your health anymore.

Whenever you 'successfully' remove a symptom without its cause, the consequences end up being worse.

There may be a huge number of different messages from the people you meet, but they can only have one of two effects on you: you either feel happy or you don't.
If you feel unhappy because of the way other people are, you carry a judgment in your heart about a part of yourself that you are not really aware of until you become emotional about it.

We run into many such mirrors to eventually come to a point in life where there is nothing left to react to.
When there is no more need to protect or defend yourself, there will remain only loving and kind mirrors in your life.
Because you have no more division in your heart that separates the selfish, arrogant and superficial people in the world from the joyful, giving and loving people, you will no longer see anything wrong with the world.
You can see the fear behind the aggression and the longing to be loved by those who manipulate others for their own gain.
What may seem superficial to us are actually profound life struggles of personality selves that have temporarily lost contact with their higher spiritual selves.

When we blame others for our problems,

we unconsciously blame ourselves.

The solution to life's problems is to discover the
purpose behind them and accept them for that reason.
This is a skill that develops when you are
repeatedly exposed to these self-inflicted tests.

By accepting what is, the purpose of all these events
becomes revealed to you, which then
allows you to swiftly move out of the suffering.
You are never a victim; you do this for you own highest good.

In rural China, people have tended to be very choosy about which doctor they will go to. Typically, they will first visit the doctor's family to make certain that the members are all healthy. Then check out the doctor's own health. If he looks vital and healthy, they will trust him and take his advice.

There is no power outside yourself that can influence you
unless you allow it, consciously or unconsciously.
Your life's experiences are all very precious,
including the negative, painful and fearful ones.
They need not be suppressed or avoided.
They are there to help you get more balanced and confident
in those parts of yourself that you perceive as
less deserving, less capable or less worthy.
Accept them for what they are, and allow the experience.
It is in your best interest.

Negative things are not really negative;
we just haven't discovered their true (positive) reasons yet.
They persist until we give up our resistance,
which is the main cause of fear, anxiety and pain.

The worse things get, the better they will become.

There are no mistakes, only experiences.
All experiences have value, even if they are not perceived
as such right away. Later, they become the
jewels of human experience, helpful in many ways.
You can curse yourself for having done something you
consider wrong, or you can praise yourself for the same thing:
to learn something new that otherwise would have eluded you.

Hope is dreaming of a better time when one believes the current time is not a good one. The desire to live a better life is based on the notion that what we currently have is bad and that we want to escape from it.

Suffering is not necessary to evolve, but when it is there, it has a deeper purpose: to help us transform what we don't like (because we fear it) into what we do like (so we can love it). We cannot love and heal what we want to discard or destroy.

It takes a quantum leap of consciousness to recognize that those who have played the roles of the aggressors and victimizers in your life have done this out of love and desire to help you (albeit, not being aware of this).

Physical toxins are the counterparts of emotional or mental toxins.
When they become released as a result of cleansing,
they can produce mental experiences of release.
Nightmares release tension, stress and even past life trauma.

All negative experiences are rooted in fear.
Fear attracts more fear because fear vibrates on a low frequency
and resonates with other people on the same frequency.
So if you are fearful, you may attract a person into your life
who is also insecure and afraid. That person may either be
an introvert and depressed, or an extrovert and angry.
Anger and criticism occur only in people who feel inferior
and try to compensate by trying to be rough and
coming across as powerful. Being protective and defensive is
due to low self-worth too, and is a leading cause of illness.

The cells do exactly the same thing: they try protecting themselves.
By becoming tight and shutting down communication with other
cells and organs, they become isolated and inefficient.
The organs and systems become weak and the body feels ill.
I have assisted people with Sacred Santémony to undo
some of these deep-seated fears or emotional knots.

You can learn everything from your body through observation, trial and error. No system can be as perfect as your natural instinct. You need to be able to read it, though.

Making peace with yourself is the key to making peace with others.

Conflict arises when we put up some kind of resistance.

The resistance is what stresses the nervous system,

and puts it on overdrive.

I can only encourage those whose bodies are somewhat
reluctant to release enough stones during their liver cleanses
to not underestimate the power of their thoughts.
The body contracts and holds on to its own waste, including
these stones, when we hold on to our fears and resentments.
If we consciously or unconsciously expect to remain ill,
it is difficult to heal.

If we harbor fear or direct criticism toward ourselves or others,
we send a message to our body to hold on to what we don't like.
The body cannot cleanse itself very well
when we go into the contraction mode.

Surrendering our personal will to our divine will (higher self),
even if it is just for a moment, allows the body to
perform feats that are not considered "normal".
However, not healing is much more abnormal than healing.
How far healing can go is basically up to us.

If you feel you currently have difficulties in your life,
remind yourself that they are not a sign of deserving hardship,
but a way to gain special strength, staying power,
trust in yourself and the universe, and love for yourself.
The intensities of the challenges you experience reflect the
potential gifts you would obtain by passing through them –
and transcending them – with courage and determination.

Life is designed in a way that steers us in the
direction we ought to take, where deviating from our path is
sometimes met with hardship and difficulty.
Instead of feeling disempowered by obstacles or disappointments,
we can just as well choose to believe that these impediments and
derailments are actually good for us, if not blessings.

You may think that taking a detour in life is a "waste of time and
energy", but you can also view the detour as a means of learning
more about who you are and where you are heading in your life.
Being "off the beaten path" may be disorienting and confusing
at times, yet it challenges your creative spirit to discover
new and different ways to get back "home" – and into your heart –
for your heart is your real home.

When we complain and feel like victims of circumstances,
situations or people, we are actually displaced,
like refugees, and certainly not living in our hearts.
We are on the run, hoping that someone will help us along the way,
give us shelter, take care of us, or do those things for us
that we believe we can no longer do for ourselves.
However, being a victim is an illusion.
You are given obstacles in life only so that you can
become stronger and wiser by surmounting them.

To open one's heart and be Love is a choice that awaits everyone.

When there is karma coming along that instills fear in you, it only
does so to magnetize its opposite into your life, which is love.
Similar things happen when there is a deep desire in you
to master such divine qualities as
infinite compassion, trust or self-confidence.
Every time you face fear instead of denying or
suppressing it, you get a little closer to love.
To do what you resist or fear most is one of the
fastest ways to gain what you are looking for in life.

Forgive those who have hurt you, and forgive yourself
for asking and allowing them to hurt you.
Bless them with your open heart and it will heal.

There is no right or wrong, just different choices. We can never step out of the wholeness of life even when we think we can. Right or wrong is merely the projection of our beliefs, and neither exists in opposition to the other, unless we choose to see it that way.

Sometimes, part of what we experience emotionally
is the sad picture we have created for ourselves.
The body's cells become sad when they are cut off from us and
from the nutrients they need in order to dance with energy and joy.

Just as you can create disease in your body,
you can un-create it again.
But it takes accepting full responsibility
for one's body and mind to heal it.

Take each situation as it is, for it is a non-coincidental occurrence
that is in your best interest, even if you don't understand the 'why'.
Once something has happened to you, there is not much point
in looking for the bad reasons behind it, but there is
plenty of reason to expect something good to come of it.
Whenever we choose to see something as negative,
we create that effect.

Our resistance to it doesn't allow us to let go of it. And so we
cause a repeat situation until we finally accept the situation,
accident or person as is and look for the good reason.
This way our energies are directed to create the
positive outcome of the presumed negative event.

You always create your own life situation, one way or another.
Just take each moment as a blessing,
even if it is disguised as a problem.
Every problem is an opportunity for growth.

Letting things be instead of desperately trying to fix things, or 'get rid' of what's not working, allows the energy and passion for living a life full of unlimited possibilities to emerge.

You don't want to change, release or root out past or current negative experiences, but instead complement them with their positive purpose. Otherwise, you will just perpetuate the fear of what you're trying to change or get rid of. The attempt to release what you don't like in your life will merely cause you to attract more of the same. The reprogramming starts with recognizing that there is a positive side to every negative.

If you are patient with yourself, your body's messages of pain and sadness can be your guides rather than a nuisance.

Everything is in our favor, especially when it doesn't feel that way.
Taking responsibility doesn't mean feeling guilty about something.
It means accepting and blessing whatever comes to us as our
own creation (originated in either past lives or this lifetime),
and then changing our attitude toward it, especially if it
involves resistance, defensiveness, anger or aggression.

We cannot change others but we certainly have the power to
change ourselves and the way we interpret what comes our way.
This is how we can change the effect that
our own past can have on the present and future.

All your 'past' relationships are always part of the present.
When something is not finished in that particular relationship,
you seek to complete it. So when an old friend, partner,
parent or enemy appears in your current life, perhaps
accidentally bumping into you or being born into your family,
it is to complete some unfinished business.
If there is conflict this time, it means you met before and are
now given the opportunity to learn and grow from each other.

Sometimes, free will on either side prevents this from happening,
and the imbalance needs to be corrected in some other way
(disease being one of them). If there is an instant connection
between two individuals, it is also because they had a past
relationship, otherwise the recognition wouldn't be there.
Typically, members of a soul family or soul group keep
meeting up with one another and forming new relationships.
This makes it much easier to evolve than would be possible if
you had to meet up with 'outsiders' not familiar with your needs.

This doesn't mean that all the people we meet in this life were
in our past, but those we end up forming a deeper bond with,
and even sharing animosity with, are part of our past. They are still
present, except their costume or mask is different (changed body).
You may not recognize their mask, but you recognize their soul.
Higher selves organize these souls to meet one another,
even if they live at opposite ends of the world.

Timeless Wisdom from Andreas Moritz

The most powerful and ultimate influence on our physical health
stems from how you feel about yourself and others.
Start looking for the possible reasons behind poor health.

213

A wise God wouldn't interfere in the affairs of humans,

for the problems they face are their own making,

from previous lives and this life.

Removing the lessons and opportunities for growth

because of weaknesses would be not in our favor.

Each one of us is basically responsible for everything
that happens to us – the positive and the negative:
the positive as a sign of confirmation, and the negative as a mirror
of self-reflection showing what else requires completion within us.
The negative things could include an unhappy relationship,
financial trouble, religious conflict or an illness.

Nothing is written in stone. You write your own history and
your destiny changes at each moment you take a breath.
However, the probabilities are set in stone and new ones
are added to the existing ones at each moment.
What you do with them is up to you.
You are the creator of your own experiences.
Much of life is about finding out and living that simple truth.

Resistance to anything increases what you resist, regardless of whether it is sickness, poverty, fear, criticism, ego or lack. The idea that we need to resist something to get rid of it is born from judgment and misinformation, and is behind the suffering mankind is facing.

Discover books and perspectives that radically dismantle that belief system, thereby allowing you to go into the acceptance mode where transformation can take place.

Life is a journey that throws difficulties our way so that we develop skills and abilities that otherwise would never develop.

You are your higher self, yet most people refer to their
ego self or personality self when they experience pain or joy.
When pain or joy is perceived as equal,
the higher self shines through the ego self,
which spiritual leaders have called enlightenment.
This balance between the forces of right and wrong, good and bad,
love and fear, and light and dark, is what enlightenment comprises.
Karma ends just there because the self can no longer
perceive itself as good or bad, but as being both –
and yet being free of either.

Nothing happens by mistake or accident.

One day you will find out that the greatest challenges
in your life were the greatest gifts and opportunities.
We are here to grow from our weaknesses, to grow out of
all self-denial and assume the true selfhood that we are.

The path can be hard and stony at times,
and the cross you carry may feel very heavy.
In time, you will find that you no longer need to bear that cross.
Step by step, with patience and perseverance,
you will move through the difficulties.

If we see something in a certain way, there will be people or
situations that will mirror back to us what or how we see ourselves.
Our world is our personal mirror or extended self.
If we perceive ourselves with love and compassion,
the world will extend love and compassion to us.
If we don't like something in us,
the world will let us know and we won't feel worthy.

It is all our making, and free will is the controller.
But free will is not something that occurs in the head.
It is the heart or higher self that makes the decisions,
even if the ego-personality resists and screams.
Only one's higher self knows how much guilt is left over
(from previous lives or this life), thus requiring measures that
may not please the senses, the body and the intellect.

A heart can open at a moment's notice
when you embrace the things you resist.

The most important thing when faced with criticism is to

take care of your emotional health and

not allow others to victimize you in any way.

To avoid suffocating ourselves, it's necessary to talk about and

share the fears we have of things, situations and people.

If you are afraid of being criticized or put down by others,

let them know about these fears, and understand that

their criticism reflects their own insecurities and fears.

If you resist letting others see your weakness,

show it to them anyway.

Tell your critics how you feel, not how you think you feel or why,

otherwise you will just reap more criticism.

Choose to experience whatever you resist in life,

and it will set you free.

Timeless Wisdom from Andreas Moritz

It is essential for you to speak your truth to those you are afraid of saying it. It is important to stand up for what you feel, and what you deserve, regardless of the repercussions. The only other alternative would be suffocation – physical and emotional.

Pain is always past-related.

Pain helps to break down stagnant karmic energies.

Treating our body the way we do reflects our spiritual attitude toward life. Neglecting the body basically means we also neglect a part of us. Abusing the body reflects a lot of guilt, shame, poor self-respect or feelings of self-worth; developing symptoms of dis-ease is a way to force the attention back to the self.

It is all about love, or lack of it. There cannot be real love and unconditional joy without having this love for yourself. The cells in the body respond to self-love with a sense of well-being, which is vibrant health. Just using the body to get by until we die would be wasteful or a missed opportunity to evolve while being here.

Suppressing symptoms doesn't make people happy, or allow them to evolve. They are practically put on ice and their consciousness mains limited until they decide to heal themselves and come alive again. Nowadays, people no longer get sick when they grow old; it starts so much earlier than ever before. An unsettling number of people in their 40s now have blockages in their arteries. Quite a few men and women in their 30s are having heart attacks. How many young women have ovarian and breast cancer?

Times have changed, and each person needs to make a decision: you can choose to feel better for a little while by suppressing symptoms, and developing a serious illness shortly thereafter, or you can change your lifestyle and accept a few inconveniences, while enjoying a healthy, long life.

The whole world is being challenged right now to
release old fears and limitations.
We are all in this together.

You can always learn from what you may consider 'mistakes'.
So don't be afraid making them.
The trials and errors help to sharpen the
body's ability to discriminate what is best for it,
in concert with your emotional and spiritual requirements.

If you try to protect yourself from others,
you will naturally live in fear.
The need to defend or protect yourself
arises when you are not sure of yourself.
Just avoiding conflict doesn't give you the peace you seek.
When you have no more need to protect yourself,
you cannot be hurt or negatively affected by those around you,
no matter what they do.

Also, when you don't see others as the instigators of
your pain and you are no longer in the victim role, they will stop
hurting you and find someone else to express their discontent to.

Anyone who criticizes somebody else suffers from a
poor self-image and is not able to love himself. People who truly
feel good enough inside can criticize neither others nor themselves.
They also cannot be a target of criticism by others.

Problems are merely the absence of accepting what is.
Resisting what you don't like implies that you are
afraid of something; fear feeds and energizes what you don't like.
Your focus on a problem keeps it there and you feel stuck.
But that can be a good thing, because your soul wants to be
free of any limitations, which exist only in your mind.

It is all a matter of perception, the way you see things.
Perception is up to you, nobody else.

Every negative thing has a positive reason behind it.
So it's important not to focus on negative things or problems
(which only makes them stronger), but to
focus on what brings you joy and excitement in life.
There is no use trying to chase darkness out of a room
in the belief that darkness is the problem or
the reason for not seeing things properly.
Instead, it is easier to simply switch on the light,
and the darkness disappears on its own.

Much of what we call problems are actually releases of old fear,
anger, insecurity, guilt and shame from this and other lifetimes.
Fighting these is just prolonging them.
Letting them be and accepting them, on the other hand, allows
them to reveal to you their purpose; you will only grow stronger.

If solutions to problems experienced by your loved ones don't seem to be readily at hand, then it is obvious that your loved ones are also being given the opportunity to grow.

What you may consider as your flaws are not flaws at all.

By accepting yourself as you are,

you are taken in exactly the direction you wish to go.

It all starts from within.

Your flaws are your blessings and

will reveal themselves to you as such.

There is a time for solitude so that one can attend to one's roots.
By watering or nourishing the roots, the plant will grow by itself.
Be less concerned about where life is taking you, and more about
embracing and learning from what is happening right now.
Count your blessings, and they will increase.
Count your flaws, and they will increase, too.
You always create your own life.
There is no other power that is stronger than your own power.
Your power manifests whatever you love
and also whatever you fear.

The best way to overcome fear is to go through it.
Do whatever you are afraid of, and the fear will disappear.
Each time you do, you will become stronger within,
until all external threats are gone.
There is nothing to fear because
fear is just a concept arising from 'not knowing'.

By stepping into the unknown, and letting it carry you through
this process, your fear is transformed into self-confidence.
There is not much joy in being afraid all the time
and worrying over every little thing.
Facing the fear, embracing it and transforming it,
can bring great joy into your life.
You can do this with everything you are afraid of.
You can turn your fears into the best opportunities for self-growth.

One of the reasons why most people don't remember their
past lives is because they would develop unnecessary guilt
for their past actions on the one hand,
and avoid learning from their current life situation on the other.
It is easier for most people to feel love and compassion for someone
who is sad or suffering than for someone who is angry and aggressive.
If we manage to see behind the mask, though,
we would see the fear and sadness behind the aggression.

If our own and other people's past lives are not accessible to us,
we stand a better chance of becoming strong in that area of love and
compassion, which is one of the main reasons for being here.
Otherwise, compassion would be so easy for us, no challenge at all.
In other words, most people have a better chance of
learning and growing stronger if they don't know their past lives.
They can develop inner trust and knowingness of the larger picture
more thoroughly than they would if they were just presented with
the knowledge of the larger picture through past life information. . . .

However, once compassion, non-judgment and unconditional love
are fairly established in a person's life,
access to past lives can become a great healing tool, if so desired.
What might weaken one person can make another stronger.
There are more and more people on the planet who are
becoming increasingly aware of their past lives,
for instance, when they meet someone whose eyes (soul)
are so familiar, when a musical skill develops so easily,
a small problem becomes so important.

There are ways to access past lives such as past life regression
therapy. If you feel drawn to it, trust your feelings.
However, it is not necessary to know your past lives,
for knowing all about them doesn't necessarily mean you
help balance them in respect to your current life.
In Sacred Santémony sessions with others,
I worked with past lives only for that reason,
not to figure out what a person had done in the past,
but to help dissolve the knots that prevent developing
love and compassion for oneself and others in this life.

There is no need to worry, there never is.
Actually, the funny thing is that the day you no longer worry,
the problems you used to worry about will be gone too.
The problems we face are merely there to bring forth
the insecurities inside so that they can eventually be
transmuted into trust, confidence and knowingness.
Without knowing, everyone is gently or not so gently
forced into a life of Spirit, no matter what happens
(including physical death, which doesn't stop a person's life
but just appears so to the bystander).

Sometimes I am prevented to extend my assistance to people
I would love to help heal from their painful conditions.
This is because their condition is already the best treatment.
Interfering with it, just to remove the discomfort,
is not always in a person's best interest.
Although some life lessons can be very painful,
they can also be life-changing.
So I have had to stand back and honor the person's
courage to go through a situation without my assistance.
Usually seeing the larger picture of things makes it easier.

Each moment is the most ideal it could possibly be;
there's no need to compare it to the
one that preceded it or the one that may follow it.
This will totally change the way you perceive yourself.
So let things unfold; let yourself be in the flow,
not in a passive way but actively.
Participate in both the up and down phases of life;
both are important to know and fully experience.

..............ooooooo◯◯◯◯◯ooo§ooo◯◯◯◯◯ooooooooo............

Andreas Moritz was a medical intuitive; a practitioner of Ayurveda, iridology, shiatsu, and vibrational medicine; a writer; and an artist. Born in southwest Germany in 1954, Moritz dealt with several severe illnesses from an early age, which compelled him to study diet, nutrition and various methods of natural healing while still a child.

By age 20, he completed his training in both iridology (the diagnostic science of eye interpretation) and dietetics. In 1981, he began studying Ayurvedic medicine in India and finished his training as a qualified practitioner of Ayurveda in New Zealand in 1991. Not satisfied with merely treating the symptoms of illness, Moritz dedicated his life's work to understanding and treating the root causes of illness. Because of this holistic approach, he had great success with cases of terminal disease where conventional methods of healing proved futile.

Starting in 1988, he began practicing the Japanese healing art of shiatsu, which gave him insights into the energy system of the body. In addition, he devoted eight years to researching consciousness and its important role in the field of mind/body medicine.

Andreas Moritz is the author of the following books on health and spirituality:

- The Amazing Liver and Gallbladder Flush
- Timeless Secrets of Health & Rejuvenation
- Cancer is Not a Disease! – It's a Survival Mechanism
- Lifting the Veil of Duality
- It's Time to Come Alive
- Heart Disease – No More!
- Diabetes – No More!
- Simple Steps to Total Health
- Ending the AIDS Myth
- Heal Yourself with Sunlight
- Feel Great, Lose Weight
- Vaccine-nation: Poisoning the Population, One Shot at a Time
- Hear the Whispers, Live Your Dream
- Art of Self-Healing
- Timeless Wisdom from Andreas Moritz

During his extensive travels throughout the world, Andreas consulted with heads of state and members of government in Europe, Asia and Africa, and lectured widely on the subjects of health, mind/body medicine and spirituality. Moritz had a free forum, 'Ask Andreas Moritz', on the large health website CureZone.com. Although he stopped writing for this forum around 2006, it contains an extensive archive of his replies to thousands of questions on a variety of health topics.

After moving to the United States in 1998, Moritz began developing his new and innovative system of healing called Ener-Chi Art that targets the root causes of many chronic illnesses. Ener-Chi Art consists of a series of light ray-encoded oil paintings that can instantly restore vital energy flow (Chi) in the organs and systems of the body. Moritz is also the creator of *Sacred Santémony – Divine Chanting for Every Occasion,* a powerful system of specially generated frequencies of sound that can transform deep-seated fears, allergies, traumas and mental or emotional blocks into useful opportunities for growth and inspiration within a matter of moments.

In October 2012, Andreas transitioned to the Higher Realms. *Timeless Wisdom from Andreas Moritz* is one of the books that he had put the finishing touches to just before his passing.

While many people consulted with Andreas on health and emotional issues, they were always moved and inspired by his wisdom. This book compiles some of those gems, many of which will be familiar to readers and those who corresponded with him as he freely shared his love and knowledge selflessly throughout his life. Andreas' legacy comprises a tremendous body of work, which he always generously shared with his readers, colleagues and fans. His YouTube videos, free health information and words of wisdom are available at www.ener-chi.com, www.youtube.com/user/enerchiTV and www.facebook.com/enerchi.wellness.

The Andreas Moritz Light Trust is a non-profit foundation created in 2013 in honor of Andreas and his time-honored kindness, generosity of spirit, profound wisdom, far-reaching teachings and life-transforming insights that have helped countless people around the world.

The goal of the Andreas Moritz Light Trust is to provide meaningful, much-needed assistance to children around the world who have no parents – including nutritious food, healthy and safe living conditions, holistic education, compassionate care and enriching spiritual opportunities.

For more information, please visit www.andreasmoritzlighttrust.org.

THE AMAZING LIVER AND GALLBLADDER FLUSH
A POWERFUL DO-IT-YOURSELF APPROACH TO OPTIMIZE YOUR HEALTH AND WELLBEING ... AND MUCH MORE!
(NEW 2012 EXPANDED EDITION - 466 PAGES; FULL COLOR e-BOOK 498 PAGES)

TIMELESS SECRETS OF HEALTH & REJUVENATION
BREAKTHROUGH MEDICINE FOR THE 21 ST CENTURY
(550 PAGES, 8½ X 11 INCHES)

CANCER IS NOT A DISEASE! - IT'S A SURVIVAL MECHANISM
DISCOVER CANCER'S HIDDEN PURPOSE, HEAL ITS ROOT CAUSES, AND BE HEALTHIER THAN EVER

VACCINE-NATION: POISONING THE POPULATION, ONE SHOT AT A TIME

HEAL YOURSELF WITH SUNLIGHT
USE ITS SECRET MEDICINAL POWERS TO HELP CURE CANCER, HEART DISEASE, DIABETES, ARTHRITIS, INFECTIOUS DISEASES, AND MUCH MORE!

LIFTING THE VEIL OF DUALITY
YOUR GUIDE TO LIVING WITHOUT JUDGMENT

———

IT'S TIME TO COME ALIVE!
START USING THE AMAZING HEALING POWERS OF YOUR BODY, MIND AND SPIRIT TODAY!

———

SIMPLE STEPS TO TOTAL HEALTH
ANDREAS MORITZ WITH CO-AUTHOR, JOHN HORNECKER

———

HEART DISEASE – NO MORE!
MAKE PEACE WITH YOUR HEART AND HEAL YOURSELF
(With excerpts from the bestselling book,
TIMELESS SECRETS OF HEALTH & REJUVENATION)

———

DIABETES – NO MORE!
DISCOVER AND HEAL ITS TRUE CAUSES
(An excerpt from the bestselling book,
TIMELESS SECRETS OF HEALTH & REJUVENATION)

———

ENDING THE AIDS MYTH
IT'S TIME TO HEAL THE TRUE CAUSES!
(An excerpt from the bestselling book,
TIMELESS SECRETS OF HEALTH & REJUVENATION)

———

Timeless Wisdom from Andreas Moritz

HEAR THE WHISPERS, LIVE YOUR DREAM
A FANFARE OF INSPIRATION

———

FEEL GREAT, LOSE WEIGHT
STOP DIETING AND START LIVING

———

ART OF SELF-HEALING

———

All books are available as paperback and electronic books, except
ART OF SELF-HEALING (not published in e-Book format),
through the Ener-Chi Wellness Center

Website: www.ener-chi.com
Email: support@ener-chi.com

Toll-free +1 (866) 258-4006 (USA & Canada)
Or: +1 (709) 570-7401

Also Available:
Ener-Chi Art™, Ener-Chi Ionized Stones and other Products

To view the complete range, visit
www.ener-chi.com/wellness-products/